Love Haunts
in Shades of Blue

Yvonne Baker

Published by Cinnamon Press
www.cinnamonpress.com

ISBN 978-1-78864-153-1

British Library Cataloguing in Publication Data. A CIP record for this book can be obtained from the British Library.

Designed and typeset in Bodini by Cinnamon Press. Cover design by Adam Craig © Adam Craig from original artwork, Venice, Luca Bravo, Unsplash.

Cinnamon Press is represented by Inpress.

Acknowledgements

Thank you to the hard-working editors who accepted these poems, sometimes in earlier versions.

Orbis: 'Cake' 'Coracle'
The Best of British Anthology, Paper Swans: 'Fleet'
Amethyst Review: 'Encounter'
Southbank Poetry: 'Remembering the waterlilies'
ARTEMISpoetry: 'Cat's cradle' 'Low tide'
Poetry and All that Jazz: 'Beach walk'
Iota: 'Near'
Kith Review: Ghazal — Moment

Grateful thanks are due to Mini Khalvati for her wisdom and advice on writing poetry, and I am particularly indebted to Myra Schneider for her encouragement, close reading and guidance over many years. Warmest thanks also to Jan Fortune for her encouragement to 'dig deeper', support, and careful editing.

Contents

Whispers

A fire through the grass

*For Alaric, Barney, Leo
and their wonderful wives and children.*

Love Haunts
in Shades of Blue

Whispers

Time travel

i)

Take a long look at this moment.
It's created from the same atoms
that shaped the stars.

The field of stars shines
from a past, too dark to imagine,
into a night you call the present.

ii)

The past folds love into a drawer,
not knowing if it will be forgotten,

hides secrets in a stone jar,
deep within a wooden chest.

And you carry past longings,
like DNA, to future generations.

iii)

You write this poem into the future —
dance of fingers in the dark against
smooth paper, the scratch of biro.

The words may not be legible,
or may be a handprint
on the wall of a cave's night.

Whispers

Her arms are full of plastic babies.
She knows each name —

Minnie-May, with shiny painted head,
Boko, in a blue voile dress,
June, blonde-hair unglued, eyes clicked shut.

Scenes appear, a sound-track plays
faint as the Bakelite wireless
muttering in a corner.

She opens the mock Tudor dolls' house,
empties the interior on the floor.
The miniature figures sprawl in disarray.

Across the room, a man is at a table,
the light ash-grey.

By a white-tiled fireplace,
a woman hangs washing on a wooden frame,
turns towards him crying.

The rest of the room is out of focus,
haunted by a tiny ghost —
her doll-like stillness.

The man and woman are gone now,
the house, too, vanished.
The road it stood in is wider.

She listens to the silence.

Limbo

Fingers, shadow-thin, carry
my sister on her first breath
across the night to a tower
where wasps circle the walls.

In a window slit, she presses
her tiny face into the wind,
cries at its papery rustle,
knows she can't get home.

The school says babies
are happy in this place.
My aunts clatter their pots,
Holy Claptrap! they declare.

So my sister grows her hair,
climbs down from the tower,
escapes to a meadow, runs
through yellow light, laughing.

Cake

Tonight I have invited my sister,
who lived less than an hour,
who has no name, whose absence
was a presence in my childhood.
I have made a cake for all her birthdays.

She arrives in a dress of distant blue,
brings an album with empty pages.
We kiss, exchange news —
a lifetime of family on my part,
a different story for her.

Holding a glass of rosé
up to the light, she peers around
the room through a pink glow.
I explain the celebration,
her face is quizzical.

I light the candles on the cake.
She contemplates their blaze,
rain-coloured eyes far away.
She turns her unlined face towards me,
I would have liked a birthday.

Pot

The white
of an overcast sky

its porcelain shell

is almost
a sphere

even the base
is curved.

Empty

the rim cuts a circle

of air

opening

to a skin of shadow

allows memories
    to surface

mingle with
imagination

teeter

without
    falling.

Snapshot with my cousin

We sit on a picnic blanket.
I'm nearly five, you're six.
My hair is slipping from its ribbons,
you're staring at the ground,
shoulders hunched.
Behind us Grandad is raking
the last of the afternoon sun.

Soon you'll leave Ireland
for Manchester, a school
in Moss Side. I'll exchange
a school with high windows
and a playground caged in wire,
for a classroom among trees,
where light stretches forever.

The distance between us will grow.
You'll become so small and faint
that I won't be sure you're there.

In the name of the Father

I'm setting out for school, hair in
stiff plaits, parcelled up
in a coat with pom-pom ties, hat
pulled down against the wind.
Behind in the shadows, Irish
and Welsh cousins stand, identities
secure, but I don't know which
way to step.

My parents learned
Gaelic as a second language, their places
of birth became holiday destinations.
In a few years, I will learn Latin.

Later, when a door opens
to a wind that blows night
rain into the house, I will cover
my head with its sadness. I will
remember how my great aunt, on entering
church, draped her shawl over
her hair, ignored the Latin
chant, murmured defiantly *In ainm
an athair* as the candle smoke
ascended.

Foreshore

Yesterday you walked down
to the water,
listened to the percussion
of the shingled bank —
the clink of stone and shell.
The white noise of the sea
full of possibility.
     You found
a pale sky beginning to darken.
A boat, abandoned on its side,
grew grey as light withdrew.
     Gulls soared and dipped
in a riff of movement.
An early memory circled —
a holiday in Ireland,
you and your cousin
playing with a shop of stones.

     You thought the future
was on the horizon,
but all the while it breathed
at your shoulder.

Ring

Its turquoise petals,
are tiny as seeds,
the gold hoop —
wire-thin —
        detached
from the star-shaped flower.
        Broken
and mended many times,
separation and love
circle.

Beginning

That morning, freezing fog
softened the white-box church.
I shivered in my thin dress, adjusted
the lace veil my mother said
made me look like a nun.
You wore the burgundy suit
your aunts insisted would upset
your grandmother. But didn't.

We were two children
in dressing up clothes
excited to explore their life.
I thought I would never look back.

But on a day with a teething baby
and fractious toddler, I remembered
days I'd left behind, how kind
the light was. I sat down
by a broken washing machine
and wept.

Outside the window,
dry-brushed clouds drifted.
On the sill a pelargonium,
lipstick-red, glowed in the sun.
I stood and walked across
the chequered floor and fed the baby.

Scenes from that December day
have blurred —
your grandmother falling on the stairs,
my father speeding through
the only speech he'd ever make.

All I can clearly call to mind
is how the white-walled church, its pillars
decorated with evergreen
and red poinsettia,
was enveloped by a smell of wax,
how quietness descended
despite the shuffling and coughs.

And how, lost in daydreams,
we stepped into the pale-grey mist.

Coracle

You cleave willow branches, weaving
the laths into a shallow scoop of air,
stretch calico across the frame,
staining it with pitch to keep the river out.
The vetch and blackthorn blossom
caught between skeleton and skin, blacken.

Tomorrow you will carry your craft
to the water, amazed at its fragile resilience.
Perhaps you will paddle swiftly, or just drift
towards clouds that look like land,
water seeping through a hairline leak
you haven't yet noticed.

Winter baptism

for Alaric

Bare-knuckled, the branches
stretch, no sign of
the brown-green canopy
of early spring.

Inside the church your dark eyes
stare quizzically into mine.
I hold you close, swaddled
in a shawl, ivory and soft.

Holy water dribbles
on your head.
The candle lit for you,
burns bright.

The priest invokes your name-sakes
Saints Michael, David, hesitates
half a beat, adds your other name —
a Visigoth, an unlikely holy man.

I remember this when you,
older, dressed in black,
a half-hearted Goth,
abandon church-going.

But even when a rime of frost
glitters on the earth, roots
yellow as old bones,
shift in darkness, undeterred.

Bristlecone Pine

Allow yourself to withdraw to a place
untouched by sun and desert night

drought or harsh winds —
to somewhere still,

where belief and feelings no longer matter
and where an act of will seems useless.

Then all that is left is the protective bark,
grown tough through the years,

and the heartwood, linking root to trunk,
will be enough to sustain you.

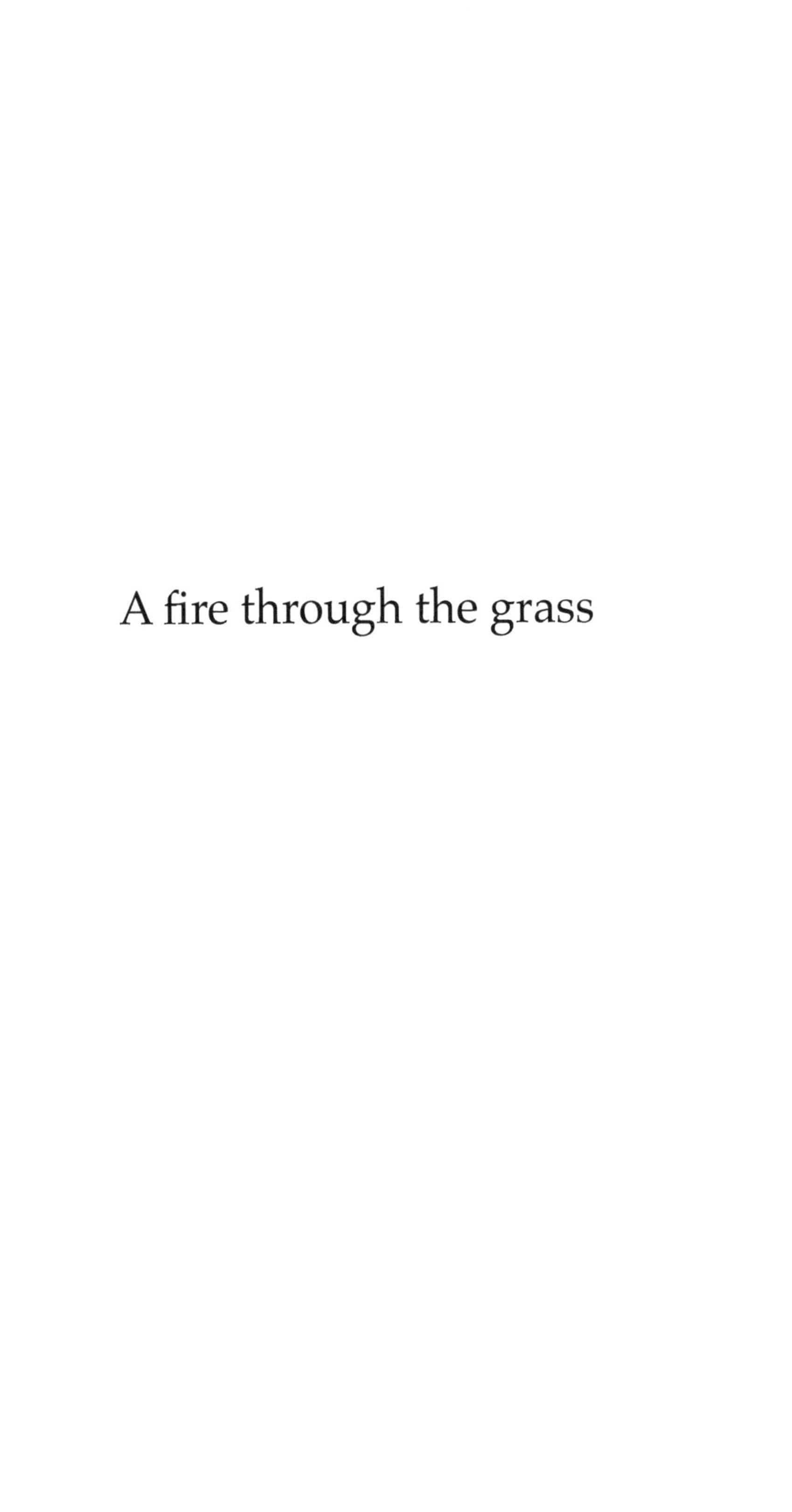

A fire through the grass

Fleet

It carries the past in the long-dissolved bones
of fish and pale ghosts of plants
entombed in its mire.
Inside its walls are hidden rusted keys,
the remains of doorways and stairs leading
to somewhere long gone
are buried here.
Think too long about this deep night
and the river will shroud you
in its depths; you will begin
to question the substance
of bricks and stone, the city itself.
There are things in its current
you would rather forget; perhaps the river
has slipped your mind
though it gurgles through a grating.
It continues nevertheless
whether you know it's there, or even care —
like dark matter, or love.

Fur

Around each stopping place were imaginary walls.
Each move the past arrived with me,

leafed between tissue wrapping a Victorian soap-dish
rescued from childhood, or hidden

in the damp hollows of the silk cushions I hoped lost.
It was always the same ritual — felling a clearing,

heaping up straw against the wet snout that snuffled
in the shadows, the voice wheedling *Let me come in.*

Once, hanging the squash of clothes in the wardrobe,
I touched a dark pelt, smelled yellow breath.

In the night window, I pulled up
the collar of my coat, felt the fur on my cheek.

Sorting through clothes

On the creased, silk skin of the tunic —
the colour of shallow seas —
silver embroidery and tiny sequins, glint.

The shadow-touch of trousers is elusive.
Drawstring gone, the image thins,
an echo in mountain air.

The shalwar kameez billows,
the scarf, a flight trail, falters.
Trousers pool at my feet.

It joins those other identities
that once gleamed in the mirror —
the midnight skirt with fluttering hem,

the scratchy suit, upholstered shoulders
concealing a weight of sadness —
both peeled away like winding cloths.

Among their threadbare ghosts,
the deep-boned self
hangs in a twist of light.

Spectre

for Alaric

At seven years old you know
that a minotaur lurks in the attic.

Hidden in the shadows
under spider-curtains it squats
behind a sack of potatoes.
Each morning
we search for it across
complaining floorboards —
dust ascends in the sunlight
emptiness presses down on us.

The minotaur returns night after night
until you grow older
and it leaves.

I have never told you
of the other creature
who brushes my shoulder
as I sleep. Conjured
from dreams and anxieties
sewn together with
jagged stitches it huddles
on the corner of my bed.

Face in the bowl of its hands
it weeps for acceptance, while I
wait in darkness
that winds and tightens
for the thing to dissolve
in cobweb-grey morning —

into rain so fine
it seems the air is falling.

Triptych

for my brother

After the funeral

The number's still alive.
The phone rings, conjuring you
out of silence.
What do you want now?
Is it to tell me again the story
of how you've been mugged?
Although we both know
you've fallen over drunk
and given yourself a black-eye.
Or to ask me, in a roundabout way,
to mend your life?
Most likely you've run out of money,
that's always the easiest request.
But, of course, it isn't you but your partner.
I listen to her unhappiness, her shock.
She asks for a recent photo.
There isn't one. Instead,
I promise to send her an image
from your childhood.
You're on the rocking horse
in the park, wearing a cowboy hat
and riding nowhere, in an endless afternoon.

Cloud

For so long you walked in a cloud-world.
I told myself you would change.

I didn't know panic stopped your feet
at the edge of the road,

the black rain that enveloped you,
its misery penetrating your bones.

All I saw was how you left the table
in the middle of Christmas dinner,

took your rage out into the street.
Your need to have another drink.

Once, the cloud lifted briefly
but the clear light was too harsh for you —

opened to a place with nowhere to hide.

You continued walking in your cloud-world
on the illusion of solid ground.

Parallel

We drive back from
the hospital, I'm trying
to swallow my irritation.

You are sober but still
you refused an MRI scan.
Claustrophobia
has won again.

Now you lie on the sofa,
in pain, but enjoying
the attention.
          Through the window
          the sky is overcast, frost
          covers the morning.
          Around the bare oak
          a woodpecker circles —
          a small shadow.

Without warning,
your inability to pull yourself
from the mire that swallows you,
hits me.

The sadness of it leaves me
breathless, although
I've been thinking about it
for years.
          Suddenly, the tree
          is gilded with light.
          On the topmost twigs,
          a flock of goldfinch —
          white stars.

The sun falls onto
the empty lager can on the table.

Encounter

for Mike

I'm there when the young man
says there's nothing to fear.
The point when the day turns,

when Mary of Magdala reaches towards Christ,
who drifts between earth and air,
nail marks on his feet like flowers.
As she clings to this moment, she hears
Do not hold on to me.

And the feeling of relief
slipping like prayer beads through my fingers,
snag on the words that follow —
We'll need more tests.

I leave you in the oncology ward
to walk into an uncertain afternoon
that leans towards hope.

Remembering the Waterlilies

for Leo

At first glance it almost seems possible
to walk across the water, the pond
is so dense with lilies. They jostle for space
like the people in that rush hour carriage.

Each time, travelling between
Kings Cross and Russell Square, I relive
how they were lost, how you were saved;
and I consider the lilies again.

The grey-blue water, scarcely visible,
holds and separates each blossom
so even from a distance
their brightness is protected.

Soul-night

i)

Spectres from your old life
reappear

but you no longer
know the language of sky.

Vowels of wood pigeon
                wind,

the delicate semantics of cloud

elude you.

ii)

You dream you are treading water.

A slight-boned fish
fins ice-clear
                darts
around your legs,
dives among grey weeds

The murky water —
night-black — supports you.

The fish, a yellow beacon,
swims into the darkness,

lights up
a pale uncertain path.

Aubade

Thin as the salt sigh of the grey sea,
dawn slips between the curtains.
A sky-print touches the wall,
the clock glows six-fifteen.
My thoughts, huddled in the bone-boat,
drift towards the horizon.

In this season locked in half-light,
it would take an act of will to ignore
the emptiness beneath my ribs.
Even so, before you board the ferry
that'll carry you across the winter sea,
I'll make you breakfast,
open the curtains to a pallid sun.

Cat's cradle

I am caught in tension —
like string looped around taut fingers
it pulls and pulls.
        Walking in dry Californian air I miss
our small wet garden and those at home;
yet in the kitchen, watching
the threads of rain on the window,
those left in the sun tug at my heart.
There is no way
I can be with everyone I love
and it seems as though the sodden grey
of afternoon will overcome me.
        A suspicion begins to needle
that this tangle might unravel if only
I loosened my hold, looked at it differently;
that this tedious day, which is already
slipping away, may later be
a time I wish would return;
the same way that the old stray cat,
who came to live with us for a while,
made a nuisance of himself
                but left emptiness behind.

Beach walk

for Barney and Nina

I search for distraction along
the shoreline, focus on the comfort
of familiar things —
the way my shadow ripples over
pebbles, darkens shells,
the scrape and grate of shingle.
And all the while another place
holds fast my wind-torn mind.

Wildfires in California flare across
the news, roar through ancient forests.
Yet all I can think of
is how close danger is to you —
twenty miles, you said —
how the air you breathe is poisoned.
The sea's salt breath caresses land.
Gulls circle, settle safely on the surf.

Tonight I find it difficult to sleep.
And, when I do, my dreams blaze.

Storm

The sky descends,
swoops across the garden,
flaps through the tall grass.

There are no birds to be seen.

Afternoon,
intimate as night,
wraps itself around us,
narrows our attention
to the creak of oak branches
from next-door's garden.

The rest of the world is lost.

I battle with the wind, trying
to keep the fence upright.
You dismantle it, piece by piece,

set the evergreen climber
loose from its moorings.

It folds under the weight of sky.

The wind sweeps across
all we thought sheltered and secure.

I hope our moss-covered tiles hold firm.

Afterwards, the sun shines —
a fire through the grass.

A small bird stands on frozen sky,
gazes at a winter aconite
pushing from the blue shadows.

One day the wind
may drag only darkness in its wake.

Today there is a lull.

Interval after the storm

You're forever waking to spring, even while
on the cusp of turning back to winter.

Stretching from a grey dream, you think —
this is an awful time to be alive.

Dust blows from the Sahara, rain turns it to mud.
War and disease rage, the broken Earth is weeping.

Unexpectedly, spring arrives. Its light,
white wine filling the garden, silvers

the white narcissi. A brimstone flutters,
a splash of yellow on the dark fence.

Yet it's the night-heart of the bush
that throws the pale leaves into sharp relief.

Meanwhile, under the log-pile, beetles go darkly.
So you wait to see what's survived the gales,

the green longing that pushes from the soil.
You're on the cusp of winter, waking to spring.

Thin space

i)

The wind that removes the fence
reveals a slice of next-door's life —

a stone path, bench wrapped
in winter plastic, solitary tree.
Across the unbroken stretch of grass —

a sea-green millpond —
light catches the dampness
of last night's rain so that
the lawn glistens with the serenity
of convent floors, thin air opening
to something out of reach —

a picture of what might be, if only
life would hush its waves.

ii)

Later, in a room empty
of distractions, waiting
for a phone call, time is
unmoving.

Enclosed inside
this border-space,
you long for ebb
and flow.

iii)

Sometimes stillness mimics death —
Shackleton's ship unable
to escape the fickleness of ice,
perfectly preserved in a museum
of freezing darkness, water-thin.

Low tide

This place, old as the Earth, reminds me
that once I breathed salt water

that the sea still runs through my veins
that my lime-hardened bones bear the likeness

of those creatures that first crept from here
into the harshness of sun and wind.

I stand in this between place. Out there is the deep
where the rumble of cod and the crack

of ice floes are sinking into silence.
Like the greying coral, the sea is singing farewell

     to a cold salt-night, singing my requiem.

I would like to be as water

Not a surge of swell and swirl
flooding all in its path
but a ripple of thin light
rising slowly to lap the walls
with the slip and slop of gentle waves
that lift books off the shelves
embrace once secure chairs
I'll flow and be one
with the shape of the room
and whether I touch
light on the window allowing
its warmth to seep through me
or trickle into the unknown crevices
of the sofa and the secret grime
between springs
everything will be delight
so that when it's time to subside
I'll trust the emptiness
untroubled by the smell of silt
mingled with brine
content that all I leave
on the walls are water-stains.

Near

I search the beach glazed by light
for the one grain containing the world
but find only the ghosts of sand worms.

Today sun sequins the waves
and the grey wrapping everything
gives way to vastness.

I prefer this. Yet the sea is always here —
in the prayer of the wind,
      the benediction of spray.

Secrets of time

The house in Penrhiwfer

I find it
clad in fake stone and chimney gone.

Inside, walls are demolished, floors shiny with laminate
and it's difficult to imagine the cramped rooms.

Then memory ripples and clears and I'm there
outside the small grey house.

My father rests the suitcase down.
A sash window lifts

and, catching sight of him, my grandmother
leans forward, the curtains billowing.

Her voice breaks as she cries *Willie, it's Willie,*
disturbing a goat nosing the bins.

I giggle at a word
only whispered out of earshot of adults,

not understanding the pain of parting —
the cuckoo's call that echoes down the hill of years.

Cuckoo's call 'cw cw' — 'where where' in old Welsh.
Penrhiwfe — short hill end

Love haunts in shades of blue

i)

Waters of the night
press against the glass.

The garden disappears,
a reflection of the room remains,

blue stars that birthed the universe,
haunt the darkness.

Heartburn, or perhaps heartache,
keeps me awake.

ii)

I dream that those I love
whisper they are leaving.

Beneath a grey-blue sky,
I take the vaporetto
to the Isle of the Dead.

Across a lagoon of azurite,
Dante and Vigil
drift towards the underworld.

In the other direction,
bleached posts mark a path
that leads to the city,

where cafés with red cloths,
cups of chocolate, are waiting.

iii)

Cobalt light, gleaned
from medieval windows,
prints the walls.

I am happy and so forget
this is the colour of distance, loss.

iv)

In blue I lose details,
notice my own smallness,
become aware of the thin mantle
that enfolds the world.

My father and I visit Venice

Ahead, is a figure I haven't seen
for nearly half a century.
It's my father,
with his pigeon-toed gait,
younger than my sons are now.

I follow him past shops
with vases, imitations of Murano glass,
books bound with marbled papers,
the beaked face of the Plague Doctor.

> But the city he walks is not this place.
> The streets he sees are filled
> with solders, blue and yellow
> NAAFI signs cover the walls.

Inside San Marco,
gold light sculpts the domed ceiling.
We gaze at its arched gleam.
A thought trickles, begins to surge.

So much is plundered.
The horses with copper flanks,
the shining altar screen,
icon of the Madonna. Even
the body of St. Mark is stolen.

And what of the gold ring
my father always wore,
exchanged for cigarettes,
was that a spoil of war?

Or the way I ransack
his memories to reimagine
a time I never knew?

The dead are powerless.

So I leave him in a Venetian afternoon,
I don't even invite him for coffee.

Oak

Call it memory, or hope of green
long buried in hollows, that makes it
obstinate against winter's death.
Immured in the bleak garden
its silence opens to a great distance.

My father only touched old age
but in his last years he chose
not to talk about his past, as though
it was enough for him to be here.

Inventing Grandfather

Hidden

If I consider the secrets of time, I think of you, Sarah. A teller of tales, among brasses and vases that shimmer in firelight, you chronicle the history of your family, their farm now buried under Pembroke docks. You recall how, as a child, your mother would take you down to the shore, give you seawater for your health. How you had your first child at seventeen.

Yet the census suggests a different account. Here is my father, his brother, two sisters, you and William, my grandfather, in that tiny house. But it is not you but William who was seventeen. A boy, when he arrived in Wales looking for work, you were in your twenties. Was this a case of romance, or love repented? William's legend is not a kind one.

Each time we repeat our stories, we move further along the grey path of memory, misplace details, embellish the myth. Was William harsh or immature? By the time we met, you were old, and I, at fourteen, wondered how long I would need to listen without being rude. I'm no longer sure what was said. The years muffle our lives, hold the secrets tight.

Opening William's story

There's no photo of you, so I'm painting your portrait with rain.
It evaporates in the sun. And here you are, a revenant of air and
coal dust. To understand you would require the Harrowing of
Hades. All I can do is to look through a oneway-mirror, re-wild
a way of life with my imaginings.

The town you live in only exists to feed the mines. Hills of stony
waste grow high, uncoupled from the valley's long-lost
memories of green.

Can you sense me watching you? I'm the whisper flitting
through your mind, the thought you bat away. Insubstantial as
light on a spiderweb, from a time you can't imagine, I'm trying
to find you.

Not even your family knows what happened in those early years
for you to roll up your life, leave Somerset. Tear-washed or
looking for adventure, was it just the chance for work that made
you decide to stay?

Let's suppose you're still walking in those grey streets. You see
a girl, hair crackling with light, who smiles, returns your stare.
Your splintered heart begins to heal, with Sarah you're no
longer bruised and hurt.

Grandfather, I know I'm inventing this. I'm trying to conjure
you from a shape of smoke. The under-weather of a time
unknown to me blows through this story. This poem is a memory
of something that never was.

A father at seventeen, rows end in tears, money is tight, anxiety
grows. A man now, you must provide, ignore your fear. Deep in
loneliness, as hoarfrost hardens dawn, you leave the house for
the yawn of the pit, its breath that drifts into the lungs. As
darkness swallows you, the world withdraws.

Inheritance

Of course, you're not to be found in air and sky. I must break the ground, summon courage to follow the labyrinth. Is that you grandfather, among tree-fossils crushed by millennia and blackened into coal?

The only story I have of you is not flattering. I invent details, project them onto the twilight of a half-dream to become a trace element, brief as a cloud-shadow skimming a hill.

Here is the school master as he climbs the hill, breathless, black coat flapping. I watch him urge you to allow my father to stay at school. Silence coats the small room. Your half-eaten cawl grows cold, polite refusal hardens. You show the school master out, close the door.

Even now, the question chips away. Money was scarce, yet who would condemn their child to the swelter of an earth-night, a life inhaling blackdamp? How different my father's life might have been.

The dark, rock-world you work in, is a mystery to me. I have never ventured deeper than travelling on the Northern line. I find you somewhere in my thoughts. A wheezing, prematurely-old minotaur, your world lit by a single headlamp.

My father will escape that starless place. His children won't inherit your legacy of shale and clay. Time's effects are only noticed in its wake. Each age a phantom for the next, only the shadows of mines and slag heaps remain now.

My father stands by the iron bed as you gasp for air. Morning fades to pit blackness.

Late

The bedroom is dark, feathered leaves
of white grow on the glass.
You knock on the door.

I dress quickly in the chill air.
You've set the alarm half an hour early.
I'm never late for school.

*

On the platform you peer at the timetable
through jumble sale glasses.
Typically we're too early.

You ask how soon before I come home
I say not long, knowing
I'll never return.

*

Uncomfortable in your suit,
you hum tunelessly.
I pick up my flowers, adjust my veil.

You rattle your keys, say
the first fifty years are the worst.
And we're late.

*

My mother and I are putting on
our make-up as the black car arrives.
You're already at the church.

Surrounded by flowers,
you've been there all night.
You hate to be late.

Likeness

Just as the Fayum portraits were not
for public gaze but to identify

Flavian or Claudine
as they crossed over into death,

so your wedding photograph, never displayed,
marked the moment you stepped into a new life.

Taken during the Blitz, you are angled
as if searching for a hopeful destiny.

The two of you are looking towards
a future that lasted

until a rose fell from Dad's wreath;
and then, rescued and pressed

between image and glass, became
bone-white.

Jug

Belonging to my mother,
salt-glazed, glossy like chocolate,
its own story is unknown.

        I have printed my family myths onto it.

Vine leaves cling to its surface,
sinuous stalks curve,

surprise
with a bunch of grapes.

        My father in a field in Italy, tired of
        army rations, mistakes the blush
        of wine grapes for sweetness.

In its memory of milk, the jug
stands on a table, waiting for visitors.

But in our house, it becomes
an ornament on a glass shelf, beside
a bowl printed with shamrock.

Second-hand, it's never
used for special occasions.

        Instead, my mother unearths from
        the sideboard the wafer-thin
        milk jug for the priest's visit.

        Flapping anxiously, she forgets
        the budgie perched on her head.

Path

Tanera Mor, Summer Isles

I stalk my memories around the island
along a track that dips steeply to the shore.

The smell of kelp stretches back to the cottage.
There is nowhere to escape the sea.
Shutting the door I find the lock rusted by salt.

Next day I pace the same route, thinking about
the people and places that once touched my life
and how the way back to them is now closed.

Across the water Eileen Mor and Eileen Beag
separated by sea, are joined by bedrock.

Ghazal — Moment

Light breaks on cue in morning's first moment.
Earth, sun-glazed, created new in this moment.

The day grows old but you hadn't noticed.
Evening, a deeper blue from this moment.

Cloud rain sea — ever-changing, still the same —
the eternal dance feels true at the moment.

Let go of night and long-dead stars, day's here!
Look at all you may view — a kairos moment.

Closer than your breath, silence swaddled you.
Gently the world withdrew from this moment.

Y, stop questioning, enjoy life's unfolding.
All time's woven through a single moment.